Restoration: Women Hurt from the Lack of Knowledge

© by Aldrenna Pope 2025

Cover Images provided by Canva for Education

Publication services provided by JSE for You

jseforyou.com

Dedication

I want to dedicate this book to every woman who has been hurt by wanting to be loved to bring fulfillment to their life.

I thank and dedicate this book to my mother, Edith; my children, Timothy, Monique, Christopher, Charity, and the twins Joshua and Caleb; and my aunt, Jennifer; those who have walked with me through this journey.

I want to thank my Apostle P. Ronald Wilder and First Lady Angela Wilder; these two people have led me to healing and guided me through the latter part of my journey.

Table of Contents

Introduction   4

Know Yourself   7

The Effect of It   9

Casting Pearls Before the Swine   12

Fearfully and Wonderfully Made   28

Is He Ishmael or Isaac   53

The Healing Process   63

Afterword   70

8-Week Bible Study & Prayer Journal

Restoration

Women Hurt from the Lack of Knowledge

Introduction

I know when you hear the title of this book, you may refer back to the scripture Hosea 4:6 which states, "My people are destroyed from the lack of knowledge." In the summer of 2020, my pastor was doing a series on "The Year of the Re" and quoted this scripture. This scripture resonated with me as a woman. I guess when I viewed all the painful heartaches, rejection, and disappointment while being single, it came from my lack of knowledge of who I am, my worth, and being whole.

While waiting in your single season for that "Mr. Right", how many of you felt like you were not whole unless you had a man in your life? Well, I can raise my hand to that question. I used to say, "I can't wait to live my life when I get a husband; or when I get married, then I will be complete." Well, I can say I have waited fifty years, and I am single till this day. But I had my first love there all along, and He sat there patiently while I looked for love from things, people's approval, and acceptance;

He was there as I went through hurtful heartbreaks. Who was that man you ask, His name is GOD!

It's not easy being single, we put ourselves in a position for men to be attracted to us, desire us, and notice us, but if he is not the one for us why does it matter? Sometimes we put ourselves in situations that set us up for hurt and disappointment. I am known for being a helpless romantic, I am forever watching Hallmark movies, especially Christmas movies. My favorite movies are *Love and Basketball* and *Just Wright.* I would sit back and daydream for that day to come. When a man passes by me, I wonder if he could be the one, waiting anxiously to see if he would approach me. I had the fairytale or fantasy that my life and family would be like the *Cosby Show.* Well, that didn't happen, so I took matters into my own hands and got hurt more than I could imagine. I hurt myself for the lack of knowledge.

As you read this book, you will see the things I had to allow God to heal and deliver me from to put me in the place to have my soulmate. There was one thing that was hindering me from him and that was me. Follow me through my journey of being transformed by God to healing and happiness.

Know Yourself

While taking my journey to get my Master's in School Counseling, my very first class was Counseling 101. However, this class's purpose was to give us the background of counseling. My professor's first order of business was to teach us about the most important act of being a counselor which is "Self Care." You see, being a counselor is giving of yourself and enduring the cares of others on your shoulders, we as counselors have to step aside once in a while to care for ourselves and keep in touch with who we are. This was a paradigm shift for me, because I did not know who I was. The first assignment was to fill out a form about ourselves and the activities or hobbies that we do for self-care, which I have very few of. Becoming a teen mom of my first child when I was 15 altered my life. I had to put Aldrenna aside and become a mother.

One of my favorite areas of counseling that fascinates me is the " Eight Stages of Human

Development" by Erik Erikson. Erikson talks about how every individual goes through different stages of life from infancy to late adulthood. Becoming a teenage mom at the age of 15 changed my development stage of adolescence, where a teenager finds their identity and comes into their own. I traded this stage for middle adulthood, which is for raising children. This is when I lost myself and never got a chance to develop my identity. Think about it, I had the lives of my children in my hands to bring them into who they were supposed to be when I did not know who I was.

I never got a chance to grow into who I was supposed to be, develop my taste in styles, or develop what I liked or disliked. I never got a chance to decide on a career and pursue the education for that career. I never got a chance to live my life as a single or join a sorority and develop relationships with girlfriends.

The Effect of It

Being a young single mother changed my life drastically. My life was based around school and raising my children. All I heard people tell me was that my life was over, I am a mother now. All I did was sit at home, not engaging with people my age or hanging out. All this time, nobody ever considered me as an individual or encouraged me to still be a teenager to fall in line with my development stage. Also, nobody taught me how to be an adult as well, I let life control me instead of controlling my life to put it in perspective.

Needless to say, my only identity was being a mother for years. I just went with the flow of life, holding down a job to make an income for my children. I always desired more but parenting came first. I gravitated to being what I needed to be for whomever, whether it was my children, friends, or a man.

How many of us have lost our desire to be accepted by people, and wanting to be loved by a man? I can surely say I have. By not knowing who we are, we as women gravitate to who we are around to be accepted. We are all created with a purpose and a destiny. God has created us with assignments we are to do on this earth.

We as women sometimes define who we are by how others accept us or the attention they give us. I know I felt incomplete if I do not have the attention of a man. If there were times that I did not get the attention I desired, I would feel worthless or unattractive. I remember one time, I had a guy friend – he would take me out to dinner and the movies; he was giving me the attention that I desired. Now reflecting on a conversation at dinner one afternoon, he made a statement about us not working out. My reaction was so dramatic, and he picked up on my desperation. When a man realizes how desperate you are, he uses that to his advantage. Yes, I did not want to lose the attention he was giving me, it was giving me life. It made me feel complete, it made me feel like I was worth it. Later I realized his ultimate goal was to get me in bed and disappear. I made him work too hard and spend too much money on the cookie. But when he saw my desperate reactions, he decided to keep it going longer.

These are the things we as women should feel about ourselves without the influence of people. We should be complete in knowing our worth, knowing who we are as individuals, and be able to love ourselves for who we are. We are beautiful beings because we are created in God's image.

Dear God,

Help me to know who you created me to be. I want to be whole as a child of God. Teach me who I am in you.

Amen

Casting Pearls Before The Swine

Mathew 7:6 states, "Cast not ye pearls before the swine." I know you are probably wondering, what this has to do with women hurting. I didn't get the revelation until recently myself. I didn't realize that having something so valuable and protecting it with my life would protect me from all of the disappointments and heartaches that I had experienced in my life.

Several months ago, I conversed with a lovely gentleman about sex before marriage. In a previous discussion, I challenged him to be abstinent for 30 days and find another way to be intimate with his female friend. I remember telling him that I had been abstinent for several years and he replied, "I feel sorry for you." I told him not to because that was my choice. Then I stated, "Why cast my pearls upon the swine."

It took me a long time to realize that my pearls were valuable. How many times have we given ourselves to a man, and he breaks our hearts after we have given him ourselves intimately? Think about it or better yet let me tell you my story. I got tired of going before God after crying and feeling the pain from heartbreak that will never end. Basically, I would get my pearls back broken, disfigured, and dirty. Image a pig wearing pearls, they do not know about treating them with care, they don't understand the value of what is around their necks. So why would we even expect them to care for what they were not trained or taught to do? Because they did not know how to care for them. They didn't see the value in my pearls and neither did I. I would hand over my most valuable possession to somebody who was not worthy of handling my pearls.

Why do we as women think that giving him our pearls it will keep him there? Sadly, it won't. I had to realize that, if I didn't see the value of pearls myself how would I expect them to see it too? Once I got tired of taking my pearls to the jeweler to be repaired over and over again, I sat back and told God no more; this was the last time. I had to realize the worth of my pearls and know that things that are precious, must be taken care of.

When I realized the value of my pearls, I made a vow to God to never give them away until the one they were designed for came along. We have to realize we are worth more and have more than just what we see. Precious jewels are not worn every day, they are kept for special occasions. The value of pearls increases as they are preserved and taken care of. Just like pearls, we as women should also be valued in life.

It's amazing how the creator of the pearl necklace strung each pearl individually, then tied a knot after each pearl to make sure that they didn't damage each other as well, and if the necklace broke all the pearls wouldn't fall off. Now after all of that, wouldn't it be very disappointing if the creator of the pearl necklace saw its creation that he created with love damaged, misused, mistreated, and broken? Now imagine God seeing his most beautiful creation being mistreated, damaged, broken down looking for love in all the wrong places, not realizing that He is all we need. Image his heart aching when He sees the apple of His eye broken down with heartaches and pain. But the biggest disappointment would be just like the creator of that necklace is that we don't understand the value, just like we don't understand the value ourselves. But God loves us so much that He is always there with open arms ready to wipe the tears away.

We as women are more valuable and appreciated when we are preserved. I recently had a conversation with my First Lady. One of the ladies in the church was engaged and about to get married within the next couple of weeks. I expressed that I was happy for her but disappointed because I am about to be 52 years old and she was in her 30s and God sent her the one He created for her.

Psalms 37:4 states, "Delight yourself in the Lord, and He will give you the desires of your heart." When I made the vow to God to wait until marriage to give my refurbished pearls away, my heart desired to have the experience of having a baby with my husband. I know you are probably saying, "Doesn't she have children already." Yes, I have children and I love my babies with all my heart. But I truly wanted to experience pregnancy. Yes, I was pregnant but I never experienced pregnancy.

When I was pregnant I experienced disappointments, negativity from family members, and shame. I was an embarrassment to my family with every pregnancy. During my pregnancy, I never touched my stomach with love for the children I was carrying. I was always left to go through it by myself, even through the delivery room. Yes, my mother was there, but the one I gave my precious pearls to was nowhere to be seen.

I asked for that experience of doing it the right way. Having a husband to go through the month-to-month experience of having a baby. The look on his face with amazement as he touches my stomach feeling our precious baby move and kick. The excitement of viewing the baby for the first time on a sonogram or even a 3D version. The thought of not having to do it all by myself. Especially the experience of delivering the baby and seeing the tears of joy running down his face.

I had to realize –when you take your pearls to be repaired they might not be like new anymore or have some type of defect. During that conversation with my First Lady, she said something so profound to me that shook me back to reality." Sometimes when we do things out of order we forfeit our future." Y'all when I tell you that my heart broke. You don't know how I used to daydream about that moment or experience in my life. I cried the whole weekend as I had to come to the reality that this desire would never come to pass. I knew it deep down in my heart cause I had started experiencing menopause symptoms and we all know what that means. My body was transitioning in the middle-age stage where my reproductive system was starting to shut down.

Giving away my pearls before time took from my future. Imagine how many women have forfeited their health, their life, or their chance of having a baby due to casting their pearls to the swine.

I sit here thinking was it even worth giving my pearls to those who were not worthy to touch them? Every time they touched my beautiful pearls they left ugly spots, they broke them and I suffered with regrets. So many of us become so desperate– including myself– to have the touch of someone, the attention, even when there is no intention of anything serious to fulfill the void of the loneliness of being alone that we will accept anything or anyone so we will not have to deal with being alone or deal with the main problem which is ourselves.

Why do we as women feel the need to move out of desperation so much? Why can't we just be in tune with who we are, be confident in ourselves and wait patiently for who was created for us? I remember sitting in my bed running back in my mind everything that took place feeling crushed after being damaged, broken, and stupid. Yes Stupid and rejected! Have you never felt that feeling like "What is wrong with me?" or say "Why couldn't he be the one?" Knowing that I saw so many signs that I ignored – just to have the attention of somebody being there was better than being alone. I–like many other women– moved out of desperation so much; we set ourselves up.

When I tell you that being desperate and moving or functioning out of desperation can have you in all kinds of situations. The devil can have us moving out of our emotions, and we can't even see what God could be doing in our lives. But the worst part of it is that we make ourselves look desperate.

I have had several desperate moves in my life. Because I allowed the enemy to manipulate me through my feelings. I went to dating websites searching for attention, looking for someone to notice me, to want me, and want to be with me. I met one guy who only wanted to scam me and have sex. But there was another guy who gave me a good conversation, day after day. We talked for several weeks before we met face-to-face. We talked for several months, I honestly thought this was going somewhere. Although I am a believer and a servant in the house of God, I knew that I was wrong about the route I was taking; I moved out of desperation to search on my own. Proverbs 18:22 says, " He that findeth a wife finds a good thing." I was a good thing, but I felt that I had to put myself out there to be found. I wasn't expecting to end up in the same position as all the others. Yes, I got a relationship but not the one I wanted; I lost myself in a sexual relationship. We spent a lot of time together only to have sex. I honestly thought that he would come to church and change his life. I honestly thought if I would pray for him to be saved, it would change the dynamics of our relationship.

Why do we as women think that we have to change a man to be what we need him to be? That is not possible! I learned that a man is going to do what he wants, and if he truly wants something he will do what he needs to do to get it. He has to want to change on his own. Which brought me to question once again, asking God "Why do I keep ending up in the same situation?" Let's just say, this was the last sexual relationship that I had.

I had to find out why I was going there with all these challenges of getting hurt. After thinking it over it in my mind, God led me to the answer – it was me. I was the problem, I was searching for every man to make me happy or fill a void that I needed to fill or allow God to fill for me. At that point, I decided to be celibate which was something new. I decided to allow God to heal me. I decided to find out who I was.

If you remember at the beginning of this book I talked about how I never knew who I was. I was everything to everybody, but I never developed my true identity, my purpose. I told God to help me find the person He created me to be. I allowed God to become my first love. Now it was that easy, I had to say "no" but it had to be done.

There were times in my life, I needed attention from a man to make me feel like I was worth being loved. But with God, I found out that I was loved all along. That was the first step to allowing God to make me whole. At first, I did not recognize how wounded I was.

It's funny how we as women are hurt by the lack of knowledge. From my lack of knowledge, I did not realize that I had to be complete and love myself before I could allow the man God created for me to love me.

I would sacrifice my beautiful pearls for an ounce of attention or some physical affection. For years, I thought intimacy was physical or was an expression of love. The connection of this type of intimacy was a wonderful feeling that was gone within seconds. Once he got out of bed and went on his way, it was over. To hold on to the feeling I would dream of it and think on it until I got the next touch.

I finally learned what intimacy was; it was not just a sexual feeling but much more. I learned that intimacy was conversation, playfulness, a touch, and a glance in his eyes. But the ultimate intimacy was with God, being in His presence, allowing His love and healing power to embrace the pain I endured for so many years thinking it was love. A lot of people have substituted the real with the imitation just to have that feeling.

I had a friend who did not believe that her pearls were worth anything or having a man that valued her. My friend's life was taken from her because she lowered the standard of value of her pearls. Because of her life's journey, she thought that she had to accept what she could get when it came to a man. My dear friend never healed after her divorce to even know how to see her value. After she finally left the guy alone, she started dating an 18-year-old and went back to the first guy.

When they would argue she would tell him that he can't take care of himself like she can. She would belittle him as a man and then end up back with him. But the statement she would make is very true. I often wonder why! Why did she feel that she couldn't do better than allowing this man who did not even know who he was to come into her life? He did not lift her, make her feel whole, or love her but caused havoc in her life

My dear friend died at the hands of this man. When she finally decided that she desired better she walked away. He was always around because he knew the control he had over her was gone. He tried to hold on but was it because of her or was he trying to hold or hide the truth of his wrongful acts? The day her life changed for her and her girl's life was the day the truth was revealed.

After concluding that the so-called relationship was over, she allowed this man to get all of his things. As he was in her house she felt something wasn't right and the truth was finally exposed. He was engaging in an act with one of her daughters. This was a devastating feeling that impacted her life forever. The man she trusted, the man she thought was supposed to be her husband, had violated her trust when he put his hands on her daughter. To make a long story short, my best friend was killed by this man, and when he realized what he had done, he killed himself.

John 10:10 states: The thief does not come except to steal, and to kill, and to destroy. I have come that they may have life and that they may have it more abundantly. I think of this scripture when it comes to this situation. My friend was killed, her daughter's innocence was stolen from her and my friend's family was destroyed.

God's love is so important in our lives. I remember experiencing God's love and realizing that I was fearfully and wonderfully made. This is when I felt his love and presence during my quiet time. I was crying because I felt his love embracing me and at that moment I thought to myself, nothing mattered. I didn't care about how people felt about me, I didn't care what people said about me, and I had the best thing in the world which is God's love. He fulfills me! We as women are looking for something that only God can give us before we can allow love and be ready for our purpose partner. We have to realize that " We Are Fearfully and Wonderfully Made!

Dear God,

First I want to ask you for forgiveness for choosing men who don't know my worth over You . I am sitting here with broken pearls (heart) out of desperation not wanting to be alone. I am tired of giving my pearls (heart) to those who do not know my value. I have decided to wait on who you have for me. Until then, I choose to make You my "First Love." I surrender my heart to You – in the of Jesus I pray.

Amen

Fearfully and Wonderfully Made

Psalms 139:14 says I will praise thee; for I am fearfully and wonderfully made: Marvellous are thou works; And that my soul knoweth it right well.

We are fearfully and wonderfully made because God used his skills to put us together. It took me years to accept this for myself. My life journey–including my childhood– caused me to have a lot of war wounds that are covered by bandages that may not be seen. Being in counseling is not by choice but by purpose. The purpose God has created in me from birth. I was given a word some years ago that the enemy had placed hurt in me from a young age that would grow as I got older. The enemy knows that God has a purpose for us all and doesn't want it to come to pass.

My childhood wasn't the best because I was always considered the ugly duckling. I had big lips and for some reason that made me feel like I was nothing. I remember playing a game in elementary school and when the boy stopped, he had to kiss the girl. I was so excited when he stopped at me. But he frowned and hesitated, and one of the other girls said, "Just kiss me and I will go next." That was one of the defining moments in my life where I began to view myself as others saw me.

I did not dress like the other girls because my mom couldn't afford it. I lived in a single-parent home. Back then, children judged you by what you wore and not by who you are inside. As time went on, when I looked in the mirror, I did not see myself as a human being. I saw the words and views of what people said I was. I did everything to be liked, to feel like one of the popular people. I did not get the admiration poured into me to counteract all of the words spoken.

But I think the worst feeling was being rejected by the church I went to when I got pregnant by the preacher's son. He had been chasing me for a while. He even set the whole thing up for us to meet. But he denied the whole thing. Why? Because he was being groomed from a young age to follow his father's footsteps in ministry. Here I was fifteen years old, pregnant and alone. I remember sitting at the pastor's house crying and feeling shameful. While his family sent him to the other room, he never faced me, he never admitted during that time that he was the father. Can you imagine how it felt for me being a 15-year-old girl going through this?

I was very naive to how pregnancy came about, truly. My mom never had a deep conversation about sex or protection. Yes, she mentioned, don't get pregnant but in my mind, I'm thinking, "Okay, I won't get pregnant." I think my mom was trying to protect me by not talking to me about sex thinking that I would never do it. But I wish my mom would have taught me about my worth, my value, and being worth the wait. I would have had a different mindset. A lot of the girls at school kept asking me why didn't my mother put me on birth control pills. I didn't even know what that was. Their mothers talked to them but still put them on the pill just in case. I was asked if he didn't have protection himself. Again, what was that?

I was talked about within the community, high school, and the church. We started attending another church. It was a mixed-race church– they were kind and loving people. During this time, my family was going through struggles financially, and it was even worse with me having a baby. My mom's income was limited already being a single parent. I felt like it was all my fault. My younger brother felt a certain way himself; he moved out of the house to live with our daddy.

Nobody knows how much this affected me, but I never got the healing I needed during this time. The door was opened and the devil allowed me to overload myself with heavy burdens, guilt, shame, and feelings of my life being worthless. The community labeled me a fast girl which was far from who I was. The boys considered me easy and would always go to me to engage in activity with them.

When I finally made it to high school after having my child, it wasn't normal for me. As I tried to be a teenager, it was hard. It was hard to try to fit into my growth as an individual. You see, my classmates were teenagers–and even though my age was in the teens–I was a young adult, at that point, with a baby. I was known as the girl with a baby.

I still wanted to be normal and live my life as a teenager in school but every day I came home to a baby. I remember a time when I liked a guy that I went to school with; he was in one of my classes. I remember telling one of my friends that I liked him; so, she called him on three-way. She told him that I liked him, but the rejection of his remark punctured me so badly. He said, "No, I don't have time to buy diapers." My friend called me back still laughing on the phone as my heart was hurting from the rejection. But all she had to say was, "Girl he is so funny." I never got encouragement from that friend, she never apologized for her reaction.

That was how boys at school saw me. Because I had a baby, it meant responsibility that they did not want. I even had another boy trying to talk to me; his mother heard my child on the phone, and she told me upfront that her son does not have time to be nobody's daddy. I felt labeled like the woman in the book *The Scarlet Letter*. My high school years were filled with me being to myself– at home with my child. I never had a serious guy that wanted to truly date me until my senior year. Of course, there were guys who approached me, but it was not for Aldrenna; it was because they thought that I was easy.

My senior year, I was approached by a guy who had already graduated from high school who used to pick at me when he was a senior in high school. He was two years ahead of me. He took me to prom which means I did not have to go alone. It gave me some kind of security about myself. His family knew my family which made it easier for my mom to allow us to date. Let's just say, before graduation I was pregnant with my second child.

At this point, I became an embarrassment to the family. I became the black sheep of the family. Did I expect to get pregnant again this soon? No! This is when I lost my identity as an individual. At this point is when I started to seek my family approval and wanted to be accepted. I felt so disappointed when it came to my mom. I felt that I had to do things that would make her proud of me, to overlook all the mistakes that I made in life.

This is when I started looking for love in all the wrong places. As time went by I began to gain more heartaches and wounds. I would never let the previous wound heal before I gained another. I became bitter, angry, disappointed in life and I looked at myself as an ugly being. When I looked in the mirror I saw what people said that I was. Over the years, I heard things like "What's wrong with you?" "You don't know how to keep your legs closed?" "All you know how to do is get pregnant?" These words hit me in a way that no one could imagine. But God had a plan to start the process of my healing.

After time went by, I tried several relationships that did not work. I was so needy and demanding because of the void of being incomplete. I tried to copy other people's styles to get attention. I tried to act like other girls to see if it would work– but guess what I realized? No matter how you try to cover the outside, if the inside is not healed, there can be no fulfillment. Can you imagine how many women and little girlss are comparing themselves to social media now? I did not have social media back then but I still compared myself to people.

Years passed and four children down, I started to invest in myself. I always dreamed of being in business and becoming a powerful businesswoman. I used to imagine myself as "Alexis Colby" from the television show *Dynasty*. In between jobs, I entered a program that paid for me to go back to school. So I decided to go for my associate degree in accounting while working so hard to provide for me and my children to better our lives.

Right when I was about 3 semesters from graduation with my associate in accounting, I was working at the Museum of Art as a Junior Accountant through my school. Another Ishmeal appeared. During this time, I had some stability in my life and was functioning independently. I met my twin's father at the daycare where I was dropping off my baby girl. This is when I should have had common sense. He was dropping off the children of the girl he was living with. Can you say "RED FLAG!" But guess what, I wasn't the only one. This man had mastered his gift of seeing women's insecurities and vulnerabilities. But the desperation of loneliness played a big part in having just a piece of man. However, this situation really set me up for God to position me for deliverance. After going through another pregnancy– with twins–it felt like a huge set back.

We as women have to realize that the decisions we make and the choices we choose do affect our family but especially our children. Because I was searching for love to fulfill myself, my children were lacking. But how could I pour into my children something that wasn't poured into me? Yes, we may provide for them, because of life– we just go through the motions of life. Do we spend time with them, invest in them, speak to them or when we think that they can fend for themselves? Do we think that their age in number makes them qualified to have the knowledge automatically or do we have to pour, teach, and invest in them?

As I looked back at my children growing up into young adulthood. I noticed how damaged they were. They were affected by me. What was the cause? My hurt, pain, disappointments in life. We as parents are to pour into our children and train them up the way they should go. But how can we if we are full of hurt, pain, and disappointment? Let's view it this way, how can a teacher teach a child if they don't understand the lesson themselves? I recently had a conversation with both of my twins about the issues in their lives. I broke down crying about my issues because I saw myself. That is when I noticed that the generational curses were passed down. I had to start interceding for my children by binding and breaking these curses and claiming that it would stop now.

Shortly after having my twin boys Joshua and Caleb. I remember sitting in my living room holding one of the boys and having this mixed feeling about my journey up to that point. I remember saying to God, "If only I can help prevent young girls from going through this." A friend came to my door a couple of weeks later and invited me to church. She said her assignment was to bring me to her church. I decided to go and let's just say that it has been 26 years and I am still there.

It was the purpose for me to attend this church, this is where I learned that I was "fearfully and wonderfully made." During this time, I was wounded, hurt from rejection, and much more. Covenant Church International –which was Covenant Church at the time– was the place that God had lined me up to reveal my purpose. I was getting prophetic words that I was going to heal broken-hearted children. I kept getting words about who I was and what I was created for but all I saw was the state that I was in.

Can I say that God led me to the church for His purpose to be revealed in me to make my life better? This is where I learned what spiritual warfare was. When I tell you I had been through so much but it was my faith in God that got me through. I was led to my church for a reason. I was led there so God could equip me for the next journey of my life. Chile, my first heartbreak was when I went to pick up my children from after-school care to find out one of my children wasn't there. It was Wednesday and I normally picked up my children, fed them, and got to mid-week service. When I got home I did not ride the bus home. I made a phone call to the police to find out, only that my child was taken by DHR and I had to appear in court. I remember going to church that night sitting in the back row crying asking God why. Here I was in church but I was still going through it; my children were even being attacked. My pastor wasn't in town but had a representative to accompany me. I remember going home putting my other kids to bed and laying on the sofa crying for my child. This was the first time that I had ever been away from my child. I remember crying out his name in the morning like he was there.

I went to court the next morning only to be accused of being a bad mother because I would not allow my son to be on a certain type of medicine. I was guilty until proven innocent. They didn't see the girl who rededicated her life to God and went to college. I was a mother who worked to provide for my children. I remember the judge who was a white female thinking the worst of me. Was I on drugs? I wasn't raised in that type of lifestyle. Little did she know, I couldn't even swallow a pill or hated to be given a shot. Just like they crucified

Jesus, I was crucified in the courtroom. I had people all in my home disturbing our peace. My son was ordered to a mental health hospital where he was drugged only to find out that he didn't have any issues nor needed any medicine. I still didn't get my child back; he was put into foster care. To make it worse, they even tried to come after my other kids, but God intervened.

I remember going to an encounter retreat where I first learned that I was fearfully and wonderfully made by God. It was an encounter retreat where we spent the weekend denouncing words and generational curses off our lives. This is where I decided to leave my past behind me and accept God had work for me to do. Just to have all those curses that were spoken over me as well as generational curses broken off my life. The enemy wants us to think that we are worthless because the mistakes that we make in our lives as they determine our life outcomes. I am here to tell you that he is a liar.

My Apostle P. Ronald Wilder gave a word that is so powerful to live your life as a single woman. These points are very key to my life and every woman who is single and has been hurt or disappointed about how her life has turned out. He said, "There are several things about life you must come to grips with":

1. Life has challenges- Although we go through challenges, we should never let them overtake us. According to God's word Isaiah 54:17, "No weapon formed against us shall not prosper." Yes we all have challenges in our life but they will not destroy us.

2. Life is not always fair- Yes! Sometimes life is not fair. I truly know that. I used to sit back and tell God that some people have a better life than I had. I struggled as a parent to care for my children. But God provided for us. I would see all the women at church getting married, especially the ones who were younger than me. I would say, "Hello God, have you forgotten about your girl over here?"

Then I looked back and realized that I dodged a lot of bullets when it came to some men.

3. Life is filled with decisions or choices- Sometimes the decisions we make may not be the best and come with consequences. For example: for many years I thought love was a physical action which led to me being hurt over and over again. I still made that choice. But what I have to realize is that life was not over, and I was about to be loved. I found a love that was always there loving through all of my mess. He didn't judge or down me because of the choices and decisions I made in life

4. Life will be enhanced by or worsened by the people in your life- I have learned a big lesson from this statement. The people you choose to have can help you or help destroy you. I had to learn to have a small circle of people. I realized that people will try to destroy your hopes and dreams because they don't have passion for hopes and dreams themselves. I need people who will encourage me and pray for me. I was around so

many negative people and thought that is how life was supposed to think. I didn't know how to encourage people, I would always see the cup half empty. I became the environment that I was around. Sit back and think of a child being raised like that. How many of us have lived in an environment like that?

5. Your quality of life will be determined by the information you receive and from whom you receive it.

- We receive information from our environment- There may be times when we have to change the circle of people around us. As we grow and transition into another level in life we become unequally yoked with our friends and boyfriend. Have you ever noticed a couple who married young or couples who have been attracted to the person they first met but as they grew and matured or even transitioned into the person God has called them to be? The relationship of marriage starts to fold. I have a friend who married young to get out of her parent's house due to certain reasons. Now she has grown into a mature adult and is going back to school to enhance her life. Her husband is happy with where they are. She is ready to move and walk away because she realizes that she married for the wrong reason. Even her oldest child noticed the issues, and when she had a discussion with him about the transition in life, her child replied, "I was wondering when you were going to walk away. Mom, you should have left a long time ago." Because of her environment, she made a decision early in life that she is now healing from.

- Repetitious information- some of our self-esteem comes from what we heard over and over again about who we are. I knew for years after I had my first child. I was told that I could basically forget about any dreams that I had. I started to think of my worth from the words from their mouths. But God told me I was fearfully and wonderfully made and that I had value and purpose in my life even with the mistakes that I made.

- Life experiences and events- we let the trauma, mistakes, downfalls, etc. hinder us from our true purpose in life. We can not let our mistakes determine who we are or even define our worth. I realize that we don't have to be perfect to be used by God.

Reflecting on my life, realizing how much power I gave people over my life wanting to be accepted. When I tell you how I would do things I didn't want to do just to please people. I am so thankful that I don't have to compromise to be accepted or please people. I am fearful and wonderfully made. I am so grateful that I am not in that vulnerable state at this time. I can't say that I am completely healed but God is healing me.

I lost myself due to rejection of wanting to be accepted. I lost myself by giving my all, trying to be my best version for them when they hadn't met me halfway. How many of us have given ourselves to relationships trying to prove that we are a good woman? We are good women to the wrong men. Some men are very selfish and know that we women are not the ones who love receiving the benefits of the relationships.

Proverb 23:7 says, "For as a man thinketh in his heart; so is he." This scripture is so profound in my life and so many others. I heard an individual say that our minds are the soil and words are the seed that is planted in it. Think about all the people who have spoken negatively against you or even to you. Those words have been planted into your heart.

Let's think about this from a child's perspective. A child is born into a world where his parents are not emotionally healed. Mom is a single parent and wounded from the child's father. She was used by him, she felt abandoned, rejected and at the point worthless. She is left to care for the child as a single parent which means limited income and she is working two jobs.

At first, she nurtured the child during the infancy stages but as the child gets older he or she starts to look like the man who hurt her tremendously. Not realizing the impact she has on her child, she grows to be bitter and pour her hurt, rejections and disappointments into that precious being. The very person who is supposed to raise this child to be all that they should be and speaking affirmations into their interbeing. All the child hears is how they messed up their moms life, how their father abandoned them, or worse. This child grows up not knowing that they are "Fearfully and Wonderfully Made" but instead thinking that they are worthless and should not be living on the very earth.

What people don't realize is that being in education is a special gift. You have a child who needs teachers to pour into them affirmation of life. School is not just an education facility it is a purpose facility. School is a place where children can be filled with dreams and purpose; they can be shown that their reality doesn't have to be their outcome. When God told me that I would be helping heal children's hearts, I did not realize that it would be in a school setting. I noticed one day that sitting in my office and seeing children in battles spiritually and mentally at a young age baffled me. The hurt, pain, and disappointment of life have been passed down the family's generation. These children are overwhelmed in life because their parents are dealing with life and not healing from it.

Healing from the past is truly important. I grew up comparing myself to people from my teenage years to most of my adult years. I often think about how I was picked on in childhood about my appearance and how children are so brutal when it comes to hurting other kids' feelings. I was not taught how to defend myself against these types of attacks. Even now, I look back at the people I compared myself to. I said to myself "what was

I thinking?" I have let many people live in my head with their words of negativity throughout my life. Especially when it came to my mindset and thought patterns. It was so bad that I would think negatively on a daily basis to save myself from being hurt or disappointed. I think this clashed with me having faith and belief in God. WOW! I know that is crazy but my head was so full of my past experiences. I would put things at the altar and take them back because I couldn't depend on anybody but myself. To go further, I actually thought I was dumb and stupid due to the mistakes I made in life, especially being a single parent of 6 children with no husband. I felt worthless.

But even through all of that,GOD said, I WAS FEARFULLY AND WONDERFULLY MADE! You see through all of my mess and my disappointments in life. God still sees the beauty in the midst of the ashes. I still have value and worth. Throughout the Bible, the scriptures talk about how God uses the people you wouldn't even expect to be vessels of who he is.

Although God created people, they are creatures with tongues that can cut an individual to pieces.

I am a living testament of God. Yes, I am a single mother of 6 children, yes I made mistakes in my life but look at me. I made up my mind to allow God to totally remake me. This took being separated from people, especially the ones that I felt I had to please or prove that I was something of worth. I learned that it is not my place to prove who I am to nobody. I had to surrender to God by telling him I can't do this by myself.

After allowing God to work and direct my path to my purpose, His path led me to confidence in him. By allowing God to guide me, now I am a college graduate of a couple of degrees. Did I ever imagine that I would be at this point in my life! Jeremiah 29:11, says, "For I know the plans I have for you." I could not see all of this, I would have never thought this could be my destiny.

Just know that he loves and cares for you, he has a purpose and destiny for you.

Dear God,

In your word Jeremiah 29:11, you say you know the plans that you have for me. I have to admit that I have made mistakes in my life and I can not see beyond my surroundings at this time. But I surrender my life which is broken that you can make over for your good.

In Jesus Name
Amen

Is He Ishmael or Isaac

The book of Genesis in the Bible talks about how God promised Abraham a son. After 13 years had passed, Sarah became impatient and took matters into her own hands. She chose her servant Hagar to be with her husband and produce a child. He was named Ishmael, but he was not the one that God promised. Then after another 13 years, Isaac came along. He was born to Sarah even in her old age.

I know you are probably wondering– why talk about Abraham and his sons? There is an old hymn I used to hear when I was a little girl called "Jesus can work it out." There was a part where the leader would sing "Abraham had a son, but Isacc was the only one. Even though Ishmael was the firstborn he was not the one God was talking about. Out of Sarah's impatience, she decided to help God instead of trusting Him at His word.

I have to say that I am guilty of this myself. How many of us have chosen Ishmael instead of letting God work so our Isaac can come along? We as women have stayed just to say that we have somebody who doesn't even belong to us or who God has not created for us. I was given a prophetic word some years ago which was "They were never created to love you." You see I used to ask God "WHY?" when my heart was broken by another Ishmael situation. "What was wrong with me?"

I had to realize that God has a purpose partner – he even created somebody just for me. But I have to wait for the right timing of God to connect us. We as women run with an Ishmael situation instead of waiting patiently for an Isaac kind of blessing.

I took matters into my own hands as well as listened to other women who were in the same state that I was in. It was the blind leading the blind. I used to say that I wanted the connection to be natural. I always felt that he would know who I am because God would have poured me into his spirit and his into mine. So when we finally came across each other's path it would be an easy process. My First Lady would always tell me that when God does something it is smooth and easy without confusion or drama. I always kept that in mind. So after hearing all of that, I began to wonder how many of us have dealt with a lot of drama from men just to say that we have a man –or we stayed with them out of fear of being alone?

I can recall a time when I became impatient like Sarah; I listened to some women and joined this online website called" Plenty of Fish." When I tell you that I compromised my own beliefs and lowered my standards just to have a man. One thing I quickly learned is that the majority of men on this site are lying about who they are. I had one guy to reach out to me, and I was so excited about going on a date. He took me to the movies during the workweek. Tell me why this man was at my house waiting on me when I got home 3 hours before our date time. Ok, that should have been a red flag for me. But, we went to the movies and on the way back we were talking about my car situation. He replied that he would take me to work in the morning. I agreed to let him take me; tell me why he thought I was going to allow him to stay at my house till the morning. The next morning, my twin boys asked me why this dude was sleeping in his car outside all night. This was the second red flag, so I got in his car to go to work and started looking around in the car, and the back seat was so messy. The third red flag was I started to see little bugs crawling in the car. I curled up grabbing all of my things. I asked God to just let me make it to work. I had to take everything out of my purse to make sure there were no bugs in it. To make a long story short, he was homeless and living in his car. He did not have a job and was looking for somewhere to stay.

Ladies, have you ever sat back and evaluated the type of me you dated or been in a relationship with? Well, I did, and I noticed that they were different but in the same category. All these Ishmael-type situations were the same type of men. I noticed that as I allowed God to work and evolve me into the woman He created me to be with a purpose, my taste buds changed drastically. I realized that we had to be on the same path or have the same purpose. But I had to learn who I was as well as my purpose in life. I have seen a lot of my friends and people who marry only to realize after they have grown or matured into who God has created them to be, they become disconnected from their mate or boyfriend. I have even seen people stay together for the sake of their children. This isn't right. Why waste your time and life on something that has long been over? Also, think about the children you are setting an example for. It affects the children once they find out the truth.

Let me tell you a true story about a woman who was allowing God to work in her life. She realized that she needed to heal and learned that she needed to be complete and whole within herself and then allow God to position her in the right timing for her mate. So she was doing her thing while allowing God to do his thing in her life. She went back to school and got her degree. She started working on her health and weight so she joined a well-known community gym. Her main focus was to work out and live a better lifestyle. This was part of her self-care plan. There was a guy who worked out at the same time as she did. It was a friendly environment where everyone was very cool with each other. So she would talk with the guy and thought nothing of it. After 6 months or so had passed she noticed how playful he was getting with her. This woman had no clue of what was going on because she had set herself apart for God to work on her and was out of touch when it came to a man flirting or pursuing her.

As time went on she started to notice more activity from this man such as he would pick fights with her in a playful way. He would walk by and hit her, so she would hit him back. This went on for a while until one day they were engaged in a conversation. She looked up at him while he was talking and he looked at her and he gently brushed her face with his hand. To complicate things more, while he was leaving the gym he called out her name and asked her to look at him. When she did he blew a kiss at her. She was stunned and confused. As she walked to the restroom to get ready to go back to work she asked herself what just happened. What does this mean she asked herself. This threw her for a loop because she never had a man respond to her in this manner.

There was a time when the guy went through the traumatic experience of losing his father. He disappeared for a season, she just sent him a text message now and then to encourage him with scripture during his time of loss. But that was the type of person she was. One of her gifts was encouragement or motivation. But when he came around he still had a playful spirit with her.

After conversations with several close people in her life, she then realized he could be attracted to her. He was different from all the rest, he was an established businessman and financially stable. She would have never thought a man of this caliber would ever be interested in her. The gentleman did not stop there, he was acting like he was trying to get her attention or trying to get her to notice him. He would stand in front of her and look her in the eyes. There was even a time when she was on the floor doing abs work, and he walked up to her and looked her up and down. She would wonder what was going through his mind, what were his thoughts about her. He went as far as to lay across her stomach and look back at her.

This started to trigger some type of feelings for this guy. But she thought to herself could this be; was he trying to pursue her? Could this be another form of trick of the enemy to distract her? Although she wanted it to be that he liked her, she still had to be careful with her emotions. Some of the older women in the gym started to notice how he would come and pick on her.

As she started to notice how she was starting to feel, she started to back off. Because she made a vow to God to wait until she got married. This particular woman wanted to have a different experience led by God for her mate. She warred with herself because she never found out his intentions, he never came to her to ask her for a date. She thought to herself what she had learned about him so far; he did not seem like the type of guy who would play with women's emotions. This woman learned a long time ago that attention with no intentions does not mean anything. She eventually went to God and asked for him to help her to move on. She realized that if he was God sent it would be revealed in time.

The woman realized that there was more work she needed God to do in her life and that it was not a good time for a relationship in her life at this time. She wants God's best for her. Did she ever get the answer that his feelings were genuine? No, she never found out. But she learned how to carry herself around him and manage her feelings and emotions. Yes, this woman wants to be married but not at the cost of gaining an Ishmael.

We as women are hurt by the lack of knowledge in many ways such as from fear or being afraid of being alone, pressure from family members rushing us to get married, our biological clocks ticking as we get older, and marrying a man for financial stability in life. When we don't wait on the timing of God we will end up with an Ishmael.

Dear God,

I am tired of the Ishmael situations coming in my life. I am willing to wait on you to bring me my Isaac kind of blessing. I will used this time to be with You and let You embrace me with Your love until it comes.

Amen

The Healing Process

Psalms 147:3

He heals the brokenhearted and binds up their wounds.

Even though I went through all of the revelation of my value and who I was, I also learned that it is worth the wait. It was now time for my healing to begin. I saw myself as an individual who longed to be married, but if I got married I could have been divorced with even more heartache and pain. I had to ask myself why I wanted to get married; in the past, I used to say to be complete. Now I know that was because I was incomplete within myself. A husband would not have fixed that for me. God had to be the one to make me whole.

While allowing God to work on me, I asked him to prepare me for my husband. I learned what a husband's role was supposed to be in my life. We as women are hurt by the lack of knowledge, because we truly don't understand how a relationship is supposed to be. I had to make God my first love and by doing that I learned discipline. I learned how to carry myself as a woman awaiting the one – God has already put me into his spirit. I started praying for my husband and still do –not even knowing who he is.

God is so amazing when you allow God to work on you. God will reveal the areas of your life that need to be healed. There is a song called "Healing For My Soul" by Kelly Price. I know you are wondering what the soul has to do with it. The "SOUL" is us inwardly which consists of our identities, our personalities, our memories, our minds, our character, our mind, but most of all our emotions. I needed healing in all of these areas. But my biggest area where I needed healing was and still being worked on is my emotions. I have dealt with so much rejection and hurt in my life which caused such deep wounds. God is still teaching me how to deal with being hurt or dealing with situations and not allowing me to trigger past hurts. God revealed to me how my emotions would have destroyed my marriage if I did not allow him to heal me.

When I look back over my previous relationships it showed that I needed healing. I was told a long time ago that men see the desperation in a woman. I think it showed with me. I was clingy; I felt that I had no identity without having a man. I did not feel loved or special without a man. So during my healing process God showed me how to love myself. How could I expect a man to love me if I didn't love myself? I had to learn how to carry myself by showing that I was insecure. I used to walk with my head down and could not look people in the eye when I was talking to them. I had to give myself words of aspiration. I had downed myself for so long by saying what I wasn't. I started to wear clothes for my appearance and not for the attention of others. This was part of me coming into my personality.

I developed a prayer life which helped develop a relationship with God. There is nothing like talking to

God and he would actually talk back. Normally a father would teach his daughter how she should be treated, but I watched my First Lady (spiritual mother) and other women of God. I realized that I did not have to settle but allow God to work on me and groom me for my husband. I worked on developing a Godly character. By doing this, I was able to develop a mindset of what I truly want in a husband. Before I would take anybody that would come and show me attention, but God changed my taste. I realized that I wanted a husband that loves and has a relationship with God. I wanted a man who could serve and minister with purpose. But I also had to learn how to love a man. We as women have made a tremendous mistake when it comes to dealing with a man. For years, I thought you had to be bold, loud, and put pressure on a man, but that is not the case. A woman has to be gentle and cover that man with love as well as cover him in prayer. I grew up watching some of the women in my family being dramatic, and I thought that's how you had to be with a man. But it should be just the opposite. By allowing God to heal my emotions, I am able to process things better. Can I say that I have mastered it? No, I have not, but I am able to walk back to evaluate the situation and not think negatively. With unhealthy emotions, my mindset or thought patterns were so off. My past hurts had me on one; I would only see the part where I was offended or hurt. Some people would say that I had the victim mentality, but I didn't think so. I did not know how to process or get past it. All I could see was that I was hurt emotionally by a certain individual. So, think about if I was married; I would be taking my husband through it. He probably would be walking on eggshells dealing with me. His nerves would be shot. But how good is our God– wanting to help us heal.

During my healing process, I started doing things that I wanted to do but never thought I could. I started working on myself to get my body in shape by working with a trainer. With unstable emotion, I became an emotional eater. I was very unhappy and food took me there. But God when said He would give me the desires of my heart, He meant that. My desire was to lose weight and be healthier. I had to talk to myself sometimes when it came to over-eating. I would notice that I was not hungry and would question myself, "why are you eating?" After a while I adapted to the workout plan and even started doing 5k's. I can say that this has become a part of my lifestyle. Now I know that I want a husband who can do these things with me.

I am still going through my healing process, but I am here to say that God can heal! What he did for me, he can do the same thing for you. Just be willing to go through the process. I would have to say my healing process wasn't easy, but it was and is still worth it today. I have no regrets about my decision to be vulnerable to be healed.

What is YOUR Prayer?

Yes, I could have put a prayer for you to say, but this is your time to cry out to your heavenly father what's in your heart.

Afterword

Life has a way of leaving its mark on all of us. For many women, the past is filled with moments of heartbreak, regret, and choices they wish they could undo. But this book is not about staying stuck in those moments, it's about a woman who refused to let her past define her. It is about strength rising from pain, wisdom born from mistakes, and hope rekindled after grave disappointments.

Within these pages, is a story of resilience, redemption, and renewal. You hear the voice of Aldrenna Pope who when facing her darkest moment made the choice to rise anyway. She has been broken but not defeated, scarred but not silenced, delayed but not denied. Her journey is not perfect, but it is powerful. Her story serves as a reminder that no matter where you have been, no matter what life throws you, a new beginning is always possible.

Healing is not a straight path, and rarely does change come overnight. But as Aldrenna proves, every step forward, no matter how small, is a victory. Her story is a testament to the power of faith in God, perseverance, and self-discovery. She reminds us that even in the midst of struggle, there is purpose, and on the other side of pain, there is joy.

To every woman who has ever felt trapped by your past, may this book be a light in your darkness. May it remind you that help is available, healing is real, growth is possible, and you are never alone in your journey. There is a way out. There are brighter days ahead. The past may have shaped you, but it does not have to define you. The next chapter is yours to write. Aldrenna Pope has shown you the way.

Dr. P. Ronald Wilder

8-Week Bible Study & Prayer Journal

Week 1

Bible Summary

BOOK

CHAPTER

THEME

KEY VERSE

KEY PEOPLE

INSIGHTS

QUESTION

SUMMARY

WHO : WHAT : WHERE : WHEN : WHY

S. O. A. P.

SCRIPTURE

OBSERVATION

PASSAGE

APPLICATION

PRAYER

Reflection

Main Theme :

What does this bible lesson teach me to do?

Specific Gospel:

What does it teach me to be thankful for?

Specific Sin:

What does it teach me to confess?

Sanctification:

What does it teach me to ask for?

Prayer

Week 2

Bible Summary

BOOK

CHAPTER

THEME

KEY VERSE

KEY PEOPLE

INSIGHTS

QUESTION

SUMMARY

WHO : WHAT : WHERE : WHEN : WHY

S. O. A. P.

SCRIPTURE

OBSERVATION

PASSAGE

APPLICATION

PRAYER

Reflection

Main Theme :

What does this bible lesson teach me to do?

Specific Gospel:

What does it teach me to be thankful for?

Specific Sin:

What does it teach me to confess?

Sanctification:

What does it teach me to ask for?

Prayer

Week 3

Bible Summary

BOOK CHAPTER

THEME

KEY VERSE

KEY PEOPLE

INSIGHTS

QUESTION

SUMMARY

WHO · WHAT · WHERE · WHEN · WHY

S. O. A. P.

SCRIPTURE

OBSERVATION

PASSAGE

APPLICATION

PRAYER

Reflection

What does this bible lesson teach me to do?

Main Theme :

What does it teach me to be thankful for?

Specific Gospel:

What does it teach me to confess?

Specific Sin:

What does it teach me to ask for?

Sanctification:

Prayer

Week 4

Bible Summary

BOOK

CHAPTER

THEME

KEY VERSE

KEY PEOPLE

INSIGHTS

QUESTION

SUMMARY

WHO · WHAT · WHERE · WHEN · WHY

S. O. A. P.

SCRIPTURE

OBSERVATION

> ## PASSAGE

APPLICATION

PRAYER

Reflection

Main Theme :

What does this bible lesson teach me to do?

Specific Gospel:

What does it teach me to be thankful for?

Specific Sin:

What does it teach me to confess?

Sanctification:

What does it teach me to ask for?

Prayer

Week 5

Bible Summary

BOOK

CHAPTER

THEME

KEY VERSE

KEY PEOPLE

INSIGHTS

QUESTION

SUMMARY

WHO : WHAT : WHERE : WHEN : WHY

S. O. A. P.

SCRIPTURE

OBSERVATION

PASSAGE

APPLICATION

PRAYER

Reflection

Main Theme :

Specific Gospel:

Specific Sin:

Sanctification:

Prayer

Bible Summary

BOOK

CHAPTER

THEME

KEY VERSE

KEY PEOPLE

INSIGHTS

QUESTION

SUMMARY

WHO · WHAT · WHERE · WHEN · WHY

S. O. A. P.

SCRIPTURE

OBSERVATION

PASSAGE

APPLICATION

PRAYER

Reflection

What does this bible lesson teach me to do?

Main Theme :

What does it teach me to be thankful for?

Specific Gospel:

What does it teach me to confess?

Specific Sin:

What does it teach me to ask for?

Sanctification:

Prayer

Week 7

Bible Summary

BOOK

CHAPTER

THEME

KEY VERSE

KEY PEOPLE

INSIGHTS

QUESTION

SUMMARY

WHO | WHAT | WHERE | WHEN | WHY

S. O. A. P.

SCRIPTURE

OBSERVATION

> " PASSAGE "

APPLICATION

PRAYER

Reflection

Main Theme :

What does this bible lesson teach me to do?

Specific Gospel:

What does it teach me to be thankful for?

Specific Sin:

What does it teach me to confess?

Sanctification:

What does it teach me to ask for?

Prayer

Bible Summary

BOOK

CHAPTER

THEME

KEY VERSE

KEY PEOPLE

INSIGHTS

QUESTION

SUMMARY

WHO : WHAT : WHERE : WHEN : WHY

S. O. A. P.

SCRIPTURE

OBSERVATION

PASSAGE

"

"

APPLICATION

PRAYER

Reflection

Main Theme :

What does this bible lesson teach me to do?

Specific Gospel:

What does it teach me to be thankful for?

Specific Sin:

What does it teach me to confess?

Sanctification:

What does it teach me to ask for?

Prayer

Made in the USA
Columbia, SC
11 March 2025